What Color Is Your Parachute?
Guide to Rethinking Interviews

"I CAN REMEMBER WHEN ALL WE NEEDED WAS SOMEONE WHO COULD CARVE AND SOMEONE WHO COULD SEW."

WHAT COLOR IS YOUR PARACHUTE?

GUIDE TO _____

RETHINKING

INTERVIEWS

Ace the Interview and Land Your Dream Job

RICHARD N. BOLLES

TEN SPEED PRESS
Berkeley

Published in the United States by Ten Speed Press,
an imprint of the Crown Publishing Group, a division
of Random House LLC, a Penguin Random House
Company, New York.
www.crownpublishing.com
www.tenspeed.com

Ten Speed Press and the Ten Speed Press
colophon are registered trademarks of
Random House LLC.

Library of Congress Cataloging-in-Publication Data

Bolles, Richard Nelson.
What color is your parachute? : guide to rethinking
interviews: Ace the interview and land your dream job
/ Richard N. Bolles.

    pages cm
1. Employment interviewing. 2. Vocational guidance.
I. Title.

            HF5549.5.I6B655 2014

            650.14'4--dc23

                        2014005255

Trade Paperback ISBN: 978-1-60774-659-1
eBook ISBN: 978-1-60774-660-7

Printed in the United States of America

Design by Margaux Keres

10 9 8 7 6 5 4 3 2 1

First Edition

CONTENTS

PREFACE

This guide is about interviewing for a job. I say "for a job," because actually there are three types of interviews that you may come across, during your job-hunt or career-change. As I explain at length in the 2014 edition of *What Color Is Your Parachute?* the three are distinguished from each other by *what you are looking for*, and more importantly, by *who you are talking to*:

1. **Interviews for fun or practice**, where you are trying to lose your fear of interviewing, and you do this by practicing talking with people who are passionate about the same thing you are, whether it be skiing, music festivals, losing weight, scrapbooks, travel, physical fitness, movies, running, or anything that has absolutely nothing to do with the work you eventually want to find;

2. **Interviews for information**, where you are trying to find out what a field, career, or job is really like, and you do this by talking with employees who did or do the job you are exploring; or maybe you're talking here with information specialists or with experts in the industry that you're exploring for a career-change;

3. **Interviews for a job**, where you want to see about getting hired, and you do this by talking with employers, and this means with the person who actually has the power to hire you for the job you want. Not (*if you can help it*) with the HR department, as their main job in most organizations is to eliminate applicants.

This guide is about this third kind of interview, the one for a job.

1 THE THREE MOST IMPORTANT THINGS ABOUT
JOB INTERVIEWS

BOILING THINGS DOWN TO THEIR ESSENCE

"How to interview" is a very popular subject: in magazines, on the Internet, on YouTube, blogs, and websites. Indeed, whole books have been written about the subject. If all this advice were put together, you'd have an encyclopedia to study. But you don't have the time, or the patience, to read all that stuff.

So, what I want to do in this small guide is to begin by boiling it all down, into a few essential ideas.

Out of all the advice that is out there, here are the three most important things to know about job interviews.

THE FIRST MOST IMPORTANT THING TO KNOW ABOUT INTERVIEWS

An interview for a job is essentially just a conversation. Let's use the metaphor of *dating*. This conversation is two people—employer and job-hunter—attempting to decide whether or not you both want to try "going steady." A conversation requires two people, not one. This is not a silent auction. You're thinking that in the interview it's all up to the employer. Well, that's not true. What the employer decides is critical, of course; but so is what you, the job-hunter, decide. If you doubt this last point, meditate on the word "quit." It's obvious you have something to say about taking this job, either now or later. (Choose *Now.*)

Even if you're at the end of your rope, flat broke, starving, and you've got to take *anything* that comes along, at this point, you still have the right to ask intelligent questions during the interview about what you're getting yourself into. You don't just sit there, quietly. The job interview should always be a genuine conversation.

It is important to notice that this conversation involves two stages. Most job-hunters assume it has just one: sell the employer on the idea that you're the best person for the job. From the minute the interview begins, sell, sell, sell.

No, no, no. A true conversation has two stages, for both participants: first, information gathering, and only then, selling yourself.

What kind of information do you as job-hunter want to gather? That's pretty simple. You use the interview to satisfy your every curiosity about the place, the job, and the people there. You try to find out *"Do I like you all? Do I want to work here?"* You want to find that out *now,* not have to quit in two months, or somewhere down the road.

Only when you have finished your information gathering, only if you have concluded "Yes, I think I do want to work here," do you then turn your energy toward the second phase of the conversation: *marketing*—selling them on the idea that You're The One.

It goes without saying that the interview is an information-gathering process for the employer as well. You already knew that. Whether one person or a team is interviewing you, they are using the interview(s) to find out *"Do we like you? Do we want you? Do you have the skills, knowledge, or experience that we really need? Do you have the right attitude that we are looking for? And, how will you fit in with our other employees?"*

Only if they decide that they want you, do they then enter into *their* second phase: selling you on the idea that this would be a good place for you to work.

So there you have it, the first most important thing about the interview: It is a two-way conversation, between you and the employer, that has two steps for each of you: collecting information, then—and only then—selling.

THE SECOND MOST IMPORTANT THING TO KNOW ABOUT INTERVIEWS

During the interview there are really only five questions you need to know the answers to. Experts on interviewing often publish long lists of questions employers may ask you in an interview, along with some timeworn, semiclever answers. They recommend that you memorize all the possible questions, and all the answers to those questions. Their lists include such questions as:

- Tell me about yourself.
- Why did you leave your last job?
- Why were you fired (if you were)?
- How much did you make at your last job?
- Why are you applying for this job?
- What do you know about this company?
- Tell me what we do here, and how you would help?
- One word: what do you do better than your colleagues?
- What are your major strengths?
- What is your greatest weakness?

- How would you describe yourself?
- What would your friends say about you, and why would they be right? Or wrong?
- What type of work do you like to do best?
- What accomplishment has so far given you the greatest satisfaction?
- What skills are you using when you do your best work?
- If money were no object, what would you do with your life?
- What are your goals in life?
- What are your interests outside of work?
- Could you tell us more detail? (This in response to almost any answer you give or statement you make during the interview.)
- Where do you see yourself five years from now?

And then the ridiculous questions *some* interviewers ask, like:

- If you were a salad, what kind of dressing would you be?
- If you were an animal, what kind of animal would you be and why?

Note that the purpose of some of these questions is not to get a particular answer, but just to watch *how* you go about answering: do you make an immediate wild guess, or do you take a few moments to stop and think, before answering; and do you then come up with something—anything—that is at all creative or unusual? This gives the employer some clues about how you would solve a problem or challenge at work, if they hire you.

Yes, in the interview there are lots of possible questions. Eighty-nine or more. It is important for you to figure out, *before* you go into the interview, how you are going to deal with the employer's questions.

There are three ways you can go here. You can try to figure out all the possible questions you may be asked in the interview—the preceding are just examples—and then memorize answers to all those questions ahead of time.

Or, you can figure out answers to just the most difficult ones (that would be *tell me about yourself* and *what is your greatest weakness?*, which incidentally we will get to, in the "During the Interview" chapter).

Or, you can cut the territory down, and realize there are really only *five basic questions* that you need to give some thought to, before you go in. Don't wait for the interview to decide what the important questions are, that an employer might ask. Figure this out before you go into the interview. Figure it out, now.

Here is some help. Assuming you are interviewing with someone who actually has-the-power-to-hire-you, these are the five essential questions they absolutely need answers to even if they never ask you these, directly:

1. **"Why are you here?"** This means, *"Why are you knocking on our door, rather than someone else's door? How much do you know about who we are, and what we do here?"*

2. **"What can you do for us?"** This means, *"If we were to hire you, will you help us with the tasks and challenges we face here? What are your relevant skills, and give us examples or stories from your past that demonstrate you have these skills. Tell us about yourself."*

3. **"What kind of person are you?"** This means, *"Will you not only fit in but actually inspire those around you? Will you be a pleasure to work with, or will you be a problem from day one? Do you have the kind of personality that makes it easy for people to work with you, and do you share the values that we have at this place? And by the way, what is your greatest weakness?"*

4. **"What distinguishes you from, say, nineteen other people whom we are interviewing for this job?"** This means, *"What about you will give us more value for our money? What makes you unique or at least unusual; do you get more done in a day, or are you better at problem solving than others, do you have better work habits than others, do you show up earlier, stay later, work more thoroughly, work faster, maintain higher standards, go the extra mile, or . . . what? Give us examples or stories from your past that illustrate any of these claims."*

5. **"Can we afford you?"** This means, *"If we decide we want you here, how much will it take to get you, and are we willing and able to pay that amount—governed, as we are, by our budget, and by our inability to pay you as much as the person who would be next above you, on our organizational chart?"*

These are the five main things that are on an employer's mind during the interview, even if, as I said, *these five questions are never once mentioned explicitly by the employer.* These questions are still *floating* beneath the surface of the conversation, beneath all the things being discussed. Anything you can do, during the interview, to help the employer answer these five questions will help make you an outstanding candidate for the job.

Of course, it's not just the employer who has questions in the interview. This is a two-way conversation, remember? You have questions, too. And—surprise—they are basically the same questions *as the employer's*, only looked at from your perspective.

Call these your five greatest curiosities, going into the interview. Once in the interview, you will probably want to ask questions 1 and 2 out loud. You will *observe* quietly the answer to question 3. You will be prepared to make the case for questions 4 and 5, when the *appropriate* time in the interview arises.

1. **"What does this job involve?"** *You want to understand exactly what tasks will be asked of you, so you can determine if these are the kinds of tasks you would really like to do, and can do. One way to probe this is to determine in the interview to ask, "If you decide to hire me, what kind of live problem or task would I be working on here?"*

2. **"What are the skills and experience a top employee in this job should ideally have?"** *You want to find out if your skills match those that a top employee in this job has to have, in order to do this job well. Problem: Many employers who have the power to hire you don't at all understand the actual job they're hiring for, even though it's in their department (I kid you not).*

3. **"Are these the kinds of people I would like to work with, or not?"** *Do not ignore your intuition if it tells you that you wouldn't be comfortable working with these people! You want to know if they have the kind of personalities that would enable you to accomplish your best work. If these people aren't it (and you aren't yet desperate), keep looking! Being surrounded by energy-drainers will kill your enthusiasm for going to work. (Vampire movies are popular for a reason.) Keep your eyes open. Pay attention.*

4. **"If we like each other, and want to work together, can I persuade them there is something unique about me that makes me different from, say, nineteen other people they are interviewing for this job?"** *You need to think out, before you go into the interview, what does make you different from other people who can do the same job. For example, if you are good at analyzing problems, how do you do that? (1) Painstakingly? (2) Intuitively, in a flash? (3) By consulting with greater authorities in the field? You see the point. You are trying to put your finger on the "style" or "manner" in which you do your work that is distinctive, and hopefully appealing, to this employer, so that they choose you over other people they are interviewing.*

5. **"Can I persuade them to hire me at the salary I need or want?"** *This requires some knowledge on your part of how to conduct salary negotiation. (Key things to know: It should always take place at the end of the interviews there, and whoever mentions a salary figure first generally loses, in the negotiation.) That's covered later on.*

Okay, their five, your five, but just *five*; not eighty-nine questions, just five.

That's the second most important thing about interviews. Now, on to the third.

THE THIRD MOST IMPORTANT THING TO KNOW ABOUT INTERVIEWS

You can't generalize about "employers" from your limited experience with interviewing. Let's say you are able to get interviews with two different organizations at least. But they decide not to hire you. You'll be tempted to stop seeking interviews because you will conclude: *"See! What did I tell you? Employers just won't* *hire someone with my background or someone with my handicap"*—or nonsense like that. A very common conclusion, but way, way, way beyond the evidence.

Let's see what you really *know* at this point. Just this: You interviewed with two employers (or eight, or twenty) and *they* wouldn't hire you. Those two. Those eight. Or those twenty. Just them.

What makes you think they are representative of all employers? The hiring world is not a democracy, with duly elected representatives, appointed to call you in. And reject you.

No, "employers" are millions of separate, distinct, unrelated people, totally unconnected with each other, who are as different from one another as night and day. They display a wide range of attitudes, wildly different ideas about how to hire, a wide range of ways to conduct hiring interviews, and as many different attitudes toward handicaps as you can think of.

By the way, we're talking, here, about the result of the interview. We're specifically talking about one possible outcome: rejection. So we're a little bit ahead of our topic. But this does influence an interview, and so, you've got to think about it, before you go in.

How does it influence the interviews you go to? Well, altogether too many job-hunters corrupt their interviews because they go in with two objectives in mind. One is to get a job, of course. But the other is to use the interview as evidence for or against their deep suspicion that no one will hire them anymore.

Drop that second objective, even before you go in. You cannot possibly use a poor interview for two purposes. Stay single-minded. Your only purpose for the interview should be to get a job, *assuming you like the place.*

That second objective—collecting evidence for something you already believe—is bound to fail, because the attitude of all employers cannot be predicted from the attitude of a few. Your "sample" is too small.

"Employers" have very individualistic requirements for hiring. Unless you look dirty, wild, and disreputable, and smell really bad, if you know what your *talent* is, I guarantee some employer out there is hoping to find *you*. Even if you're crazy, there's some employer crazier than you.

So determine ahead of time that if you don't get hired in your first interviews, you will keep going. Even if you've been interviewing for two years, and no one has hired you yet, you must keep going. Don't ever give up. Don't ever give up.

Rethink your strategy. Rethink your approach. Learn new tricks. Read the latest version of *What Color Is Your Parachute?* Do the self-inventory there (the Flower Exercise), rethink who you are and what you have to offer. Some employers out there *do* want you. Yes, you. But it's not their job to find you. It's your job to find *them*.

It will help you in your search if you notice that there is a big difference between **large employers** (those with hundreds or thousands of employees) and **small employers** (alternately defined as those with 25 or fewer employees, those with 50 or fewer employees, or—the most common definition—those with 100 or fewer employees).

The chief difference is that large employers are harder to reach, especially if the-person-who-has-the-power-to-hire-you (for the job you want) is in some deep inner chamber of that company, and the company's phone has a voice menu with eighteen infuriating layers. Don't think your interviewing experience with small employers will necessarily be at all like the labyrinth you encountered with large ones.

Also, it will help you in your search if you notice that there is a big difference between **new companies** or enterprises, and those that have been around **for some time**, as far as hiring is concerned. A study reported in *Time* magazine found that small companies (100 or fewer employees) that were less than six years old created 4.7 million jobs in the year studied, while older small firms created only 3.2 million jobs. So if your interviews haven't gone well, try concentrating your search on *newer* small firms. Don't think your interviewing experience with new companies will necessarily be at all like the rejection you experienced when you interviewed with older ones.

SUMMARY

Okay, there you have the three most important things about interviewing. The three that stand out amid a virtual mountain of advice about job interviews that is out there:

An interview is essentially just a two-way conversation.

There are only five questions you really need to know the answer to, and only five questions you need to ask yourself.

And, you can't generalize about "employers," from your experience with interviewing.

Three. Mark them well, and now let's move on.

2 BEFORE THE INTERVIEW

THE CRUCIAL PART OF THE INTERVIEW

Some of you will be surprised to see this chapter. What? There's something you're supposed to do before you go in for the interview? Yes, indeed, there is. In fact, the period before the interview is in many ways just as important as the interview itself.

Now, life and chance being what it is, it's possible that if you just show up for an interview without any thought or preparation beforehand, you might get a terrific job offer, through sheer luck.

Much more likely it is that you will just get nothin'. And you will, in such a case, richly deserve it. In the hiring game there is only one word for job-hunters who don't prepare for the interview, but just show up. That word is *lazy*.

No employer wants to hire someone who is lazy. Unless they're lazier than you.

So, if you know what you are doing, you will take time before the interview to think through some stuff, and find out some stuff.

The latter is of course called "research." There are four things you can research before the day of the interview: the organization, the job, the interviewer(s), and the salary. Each of these, and all of these, will increase your chances of getting hired. In other words, you can be richly repaid for the time you spend on these, before the interview.

RESEARCHING THE ORGANIZATION BEFORE THE INTERVIEW

You know, of course, that the employer comes into the interview curious about you.

But the little secret about interviewing is that in most cases, the employer is even more curious to find out what you know about them.

Why? Because organizations love to be loved. If you've gone to the trouble of finding out as much as you can about them, before you interview with them, they will be flattered and impressed, believe me.

Most job-hunters never go to this amount of trouble. Most just walk in the door, knowing nothing about the organization. I have a friend who ran a large organization in Virginia; he said to me, "I'm so tired of people coming in here, saying, *Uh, what do you do here?* that the next person who comes in here and has done some prior research on us, I'm going to offer a job." He called me a week later to say, "I did it."

So don't skip this step. It may make the difference between your being hired, or not being hired. I recently talked to an expert who does nothing but hiring for client companies. I asked him the chief reason why he turns people down. He said it was this.

They come to the interview knowing nothing about the organization. So they're toast,[*] after the first five minutes. Mostly nobody ever tells them why.

So, don't be toast. Find out everything you can about the organization where you are interviewing, before you go to the interview.

Google them.

Go to their website if they have one, and read everything that is there under the heading "About Us," or "News Releases." Many job-hunters or career-changers think that every organization, company, or nonprofit has its own website, these days. Not true. Sometimes they do, sometimes they don't. It often has to do with the size of the place, its access to a good Web designer, its desperation for customers, etc. Easy way to find out: If you have access to the Internet, type the name of the place into your favorite search engine (Google, Bing, or whatever) and see what that turns up. Try more than one search engine.

If you're on LinkedIn (and you'd better be) find out who among your Links either works or used to work there. Then contact them, and ask them questions about the organization.

If the organization is local, and your town has a public library, ask your local librarian for help in finding any news clippings or other information about the place.

And, finally, ask all your friends if they know anyone who ever worked there, or works there still, so you can take them to lunch or tea or Starbucks and find out any inside stories, before you approach the interview.

---

*Slang, common in the United States, defined for my overseas friends as to be doomed, ruined, or in trouble: If you're late to work again, you're toast!

If you ask to talk to someone, during this research, keep one thing in mind above all else: the time. When you ask for the chat, remove their dread of how long this is going to take, by specifying how much time you are asking of them. Make it some oddball period, like "I need nineteen minutes of your time" (*twenty* sounds vague, *nineteen* sounds precise—like you are really serious). Then keep that commitment as though your life depended on it. Nineteen minutes. Not one minute more.

If you have a smartphone that allows you to select "vibrate" without any sound, set its timer before your chat with them begins. Set it for *seventeen* minutes (that leaves you two minutes to wrap up). Activate the timer as you sit down to talk. And keep the phone in a pocket or location near you, where you can feel the vibration, when it comes. Tap it off, and prepare to end the talk, saying, "*I said I would only take nineteen minutes of your time, and I like to honor my agreements.*" This will always make a huge impression on the person you talk to; never know who else they'll tell! You are a woman, or man, of your word!! That's a golden reputation to have.

RESEARCHING THE JOB BEFORE THE INTERVIEW

What is it you want to know about the job, before (not just during) the interview? You want to know what it takes to be successful at it. And, what would cause you to fail at it.

And, more importantly, if you feel you have some kind of handicap, you want to know if that handicap will interfere with your doing that job. This is covered in Appendix A: Handicaps.

And let's face it, your best source of information here would be the person who previously held the job that you're going in to interview for. The next best source of information about the job would be her or his supervisor. But unless you stumble across them by sheerest accident, finding out their names and then getting in contact with them may take more time than it is worth. You could try LinkedIn, and ask it to tell you the people in your network who work for that organization in other departments. They may know *something* about that job.

But the basic problem here is the job's title. There are as many different job titles as there are fishes in the sea, some of them for the same exact job. Research is based on titles. Absent any universal understanding of what lies beneath a particular job title, you may not be able to find out much beforehand. In which case, you're going to have to go in blind.

But, if that's the case, you should determine to do this research early in the interview. My two favorite questions a job hunter can ask here are, *Can you help me understand exactly what this job involves?* and *If you had to fire someone from this job in the past, present, or future, it would be because they couldn't do what? What is it they lacked that you were hoping for?*

RESEARCHING THE INTERVIEWER(S) BEFORE THE INTERVIEW

This used to be much more important than it is now. The theory was that if you could find out something you both have in common, then that would help create rapport between you. Say, you both liked boating. Or whatever. You were advised, in the old days, to look around the office as you went in, look at the pictures on the wall, the various displays there, and so forth. You were advised to look up the interviewer's biography, if you could find it, and look for anything you two had in common:

born in the same state, went to the same schools, majored in the same major, or whatever.

All of this presumed an interview in an old-style office, not a glass cubicle or factory floor, and it presumed the interview was with just one boss, not with a whole committee. The interviewing landscape has gotten much more complex since "the good old days."

Still, the overarching idea remains true: employers tend to hire friends. If you weren't a friend when you came in for the interview, it sure helps if the employer thinks of you as akin to a friend, at the end. Friends share things in common. So stay alert. Watch for anything you and the-person-who-has-the-power-to-hire-you share in common, as the interview unfolds.

RESEARCHING SALARY RANGES BEFORE THE INTERVIEW

It says "researching," but is that the most important thing you do, concerning salary, before you go to the interview? No, it's not. Research comes second. First comes strategy. You need to think out, beforehand, what strategy you're going to use, where salary is concerned. And fortunately we know, from decades of experimentation, what the most successful strategy is.

The most successful strategy is a promise. A promise that you make to yourself. And that promise is, "I will not let salary be discussed—if I can help it—until the end of the interview or series of interviews there."

Let me hammer this home: it is in your best interest to *not* discuss salary until all of the following conditions have been fulfilled:

- Not until they've gotten to know you, at your best, so they can see how you stand out above the other applicants, and therefore how you're worth more than they would pay *them*.

- Not until you've gotten to know them, as completely as you can, so you can tell if this really is a place where you want to work.
- Not until you've found out exactly what the job entails.
- Not until they've had a chance to find out how well you match their job requirements.
- Not until you're in the final interview at that place, after maybe a whole series of interviews, for that job.
- Not until you've decided, "I *really* would like to work here."
- Not until they've conveyed to you their feelings, such as: "Well that's good, because we want you." Or, better yet:
- Not until they've conveyed the feeling, "We've *got* to have you."

If you'd prefer this be put in the form of a diagram, here it is:

WHEN TO NEGOTIATE SALARY*

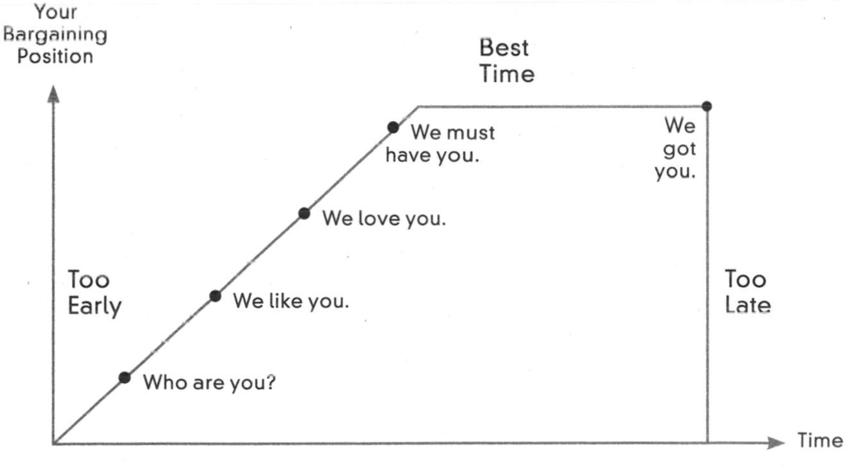

*Reprinted by permission of Paul Hellman, author of *Ready, Aim, You're Hired!* and president of Express Potential (www.expresspotential.com). All rights reserved.

It all boils down to this: you need to postpone discussion of salary just as long as possible, because if you really shine during the interview, they may—at the end—offer you a higher salary than they originally had in mind when the interview began. And this is particularly the case when the interview has gone so well that they're maybe even *determined* to obtain you.

But let's be mentally prepared for any eventuality. What if they try to raise the issue earlier, say, at the very start of the interview, asking (innocently), *"What kind of salary are you looking for?"* What are you going to do, then? Well, there are some strategies you can be prepared to use; maybe they'll work, maybe they won't. But they're certainly worth trying.

Strategy #1: If the employer seems like a kindly man or woman, your best and most tactful reply would be: *"Until you've decided you definitely want me, and I've decided I definitely could help you with your tasks or projects here, I feel any discussion of salary is premature."*

That will work, in most cases. There are instances, however, where that doesn't work. Then you need:

Strategy #2: You may be face-to-face with an employer who demands within the first two minutes of the interview to know what salary you are looking for. This is not good, especially since 2008, as employers can afford to be really picky, since—in their minds—there is now a plentiful backlog of job-hunters to choose from. So, you may need a backup response, such as: *"I'll gladly answer that, but could you first help me understand what this job involves?"*

That is a good response, in most cases. But what if that too doesn't work? Then you'll need to fall back on:

Strategy #3: The employer, with rising voice, says, *"Come, come, don't play games with me. I want to know what salary you're looking for."*

Okay, that's that. You have to come clean. But you shouldn't mention a single figure; instead you should answer in terms of *a range.* For example, *"I'm looking for a salary in the range of $35,000 to $45,000 a year."*

If that still doesn't satisfy them, then clearly you are being interviewed by an employer who has no negotiation in mind. Their beginning figure is their ending figure. No negotiation is possible.* This happens, when it does, because many employers since 2008 are making salary their major criterion for deciding who to hire, and who not to hire. It's an old game: *can I get the help I need, cheaper?* In which case, between two equally qualified candidates, the one who is willing to work for the least pay, wins. And *that* is *that!*

If you run into this situation, you have two choices. The first is to finish the interview, but resolve that this isn't the kind of place you want to work, because if they're inflexible in this, what else will they be inflexible about, once you take the job?

On the other hand, if you're flat broke and you need this job—any job—desperately, you will have no choice but to give in. Ask what salary they have in mind, and make your decision. (Of course you can always try postponing your decision a day or so, by saying, "I need a little time, to think about this.")

---

*One job-hunter said his interviews always began with the salary question, and no matter what he answered, that ended the interview. Turned out, this job-hunter was doing all the interviewing over the phone. That was the problem. Once he went face-to-face, salary was no longer the first thing discussed in the interview.

However, all the foregoing is merely the worst-case scenario. Hopefully, things won't go this badly, where you feel so powerless.

But the overarching message here is this: *before you go in to the interview*, think all this through. Don't wait. And make that promise to yourself. Please.

Okay, we're done with strategy. You've thought it out beforehand. You're prepared. In fact, you're prepared to excel the other people they're interviewing. So we can turn now to the other thing, the *research*.

Why do you want to research salaries, prior to the interview? Well, maybe you don't. This whole idea seems a bit outdated, given that employers since the Great Recession are pretty determined to pay the lowest salary they can get away with, and—given the large pool of unemployed job-hunters that is out there right now—they can get away with *a lot*. Still, that's only true *sometimes*.

If you have talents or experience that is much in demand—let's say you are a whiz at accounting, or at applied mathematics—then the power equation shifts. In that case, you need to know what the going rates are for the work you are skilled at doing, so that if the employer lowballs you, you will know it.

You'll know it because you've taken the time and trouble to do the research, and you've found out what the typical salaries are for that job in that industry in that part of the country. Then in the interview if the employer makes an offer, but comes in too low, you can help *educate* them. (I'm being kind.)

Okay, then, how do you do this research?

On the Internet—at home or at your local library or Internet café—you can research typical salaries for the kind of job you are interviewing for.

Here are some free sites that may give you just what you're looking for:

- http://jobstar.org/tools/salary/index.cfm: This site is a treasure trove. It links to three hundred different sites that maintain salary lists, and joy, joy, it is kept updated. It's one of the largest and most complete lists of salary reviews on the Web, maintained by a genius named Mary Ellen Mort.

- www.salary.com: The most visited of all the salary-specific job sites, with a wide variety of information about salaries. It was started by Kent Plunkett, but acquired by Kenexa Corporation in August 2010. It has expanded a lot, over the years. Roll over the green navigation bar at the top to see all its resources.

- www.bls.gov/ooh: The Bureau of Labor Statistics' survey of salaries in individual occupations, from the *Occupational Outlook Handbook* 2012–2013. (The 2013–2014 edition is in print, as of this writing, so I expect this online site will be updated soon.)

- http://stats.bls.gov/oes/oes_emp.htm: The Bureau of Labor Statistics' survey of salaries in individual industries (it's a companion piece to the *Occupational Outlook Handbook*). Over a period of three years, it surveys 1.2 million establishments to get their figures.

- www.salaryexpert.com: When you need a salary expert, it makes sense to go to "the Salary Expert." Lots of stuff on the subject of salaries here, including a free "Salary Report" for hundreds of job titles, varying by area, skill level, and experience. It also has some salary calculators. I find the site a little complicated to navigate, but maybe that's just me.

- www.glassdoor.com/Salaries/index.htm: This site allows you to search based on location and job title or company.

So, there's your list. And it's only a sampling. But do give this research whatever time you can, so that you can then go to the interview satisfied that you won't let the employer put one over on you, when you're talking salary. *"Oh, but that's what this kind of job pays."* *"With all due respect, Sir or Madam [as the case may be], that's not true. I researched it."*

For further help with this, see Appendix B.

Now, on to one more preparation you might want to make.

PRACTICING "THE ELEVATOR SPEECH"

This is an exercise where you rehearse what you're planning to say about yourself in the interview. Typically, it is your answer to the employer's opening gambit: *"Well, tell me about yourself."*

The problem is that under stressful conditions, people often tend to run off at the mouth. So, this exercise sets limits. It pretends that your interview is in a downtown high-rise building, and you've bumped into the interviewer early. In the elevator at the ground floor. The discipline is, Can you define for them who you are and what your value is to them, in the length of time the elevator takes to reach the top floor? It is assumed that this takes 30 seconds.

People who teach this idea call it by various names—the elevator speech, the elevator pitch, or the elevator statement—and they will sometimes allow the imaginary elevator ride to last for two minutes *(where are they? in the Khalifa Tower in Dubai?).*

Well, never mind. Job-hunters generally hate this exercise, whatever its name or form; it creates anxiety, at the very thought of trying to compress everything about yourself into such a short period.

Fortunately, that's not what this exercise asks you to do. In the thirty-second speech you are *not* expected to summarize all that you are—where you were born, where you went to school, what jobs you've had thus far, your family history, places you've visited around the world, or what you two share in common.

It is expected to be a more limited and focused summary about you. You're expected to briefly mention your understanding of The Job you're coming to interview for, and then only the stuff about You that's relevant *to that job*—the experience and qualifications you have that make you an excellent candidate *for that job*.

Rehearse just that. Nothing more. And keep rehearsing it, until you can say it in thirty seconds.

This presumes, of course, that you've done enough research to know what the job is that you're applying for; some job-hunters just rehearse a generic elevator speech about why they'd be a good candidate for *any* job. That's not the point. The employer is looking for a match. Between the job, and you. Can you summarize in thirty seconds why you are that match?

That's the elevator speech.

That's the exact answer you're expected to give when you're asked that dreaded question in the interview: *tell me about yourself.*

HOW TO DRESS?

Experts will give you many different answers to this question. The advice will range from *"dress up as if you were going to a formal wedding"* to *"dress in the style you see the employees at that place dressing"* to *"don't wear a suit to an interview with a young group of techies or design types"* to *"dress like an executive even if you're going to apply for a job on a road gang"* to *"wear the clothes you would wear day by day if you get the job"* (but I'd dump the hard hat, if I were you).

Dirty little secret: These experts don't really know *what* you should wear to *that* interview with *that* employer. They're just generalizing. I mean, guessing.

Personally, I think you should be able to dress any way you want to, and then go find an employer who agrees. (*"Hermit seeks hermit employer."*) But that may take you more time to find than it's worth.

So, if you want to be ready to interview with any and every employer, then you'd probably better pay attention to those generalizations. Which, for better or for worse, add up to this: *dress to look your best, but if you never ever dress up the other 364 days of the year, and you feel horribly self-conscious in a suit and tie, or business dress, then dial it back one level—wear nice-looking clothes that you're comfortable in (say, pantsuit, or pants/sport coat/open-neck shirt) so you can keep your consciousness on the interview and not on your appearance. Just pick out the outfit long before you interview, so that there's time for you to get it cleaned and pressed, plus get your shoes all ready—shined if the shoes take a shine, making sure they're not dusty or horribly scuffed. And be sure there's not a hole in the bottom of your shoe. Presidential candidate Adlai Stevenson is said to have lost his bid for the job because of that.*

Here are other suggestions about dressing for the interview:

1. First of all, get a good night's sleep prior to the day of the interview. You can always fix everything but your face. If you're dead tired, your face will show it. If you're feeling rung out, your face will show it. If you're low on energy, your face will show it. Fix your face. Get a good night's sleep for several days before the interview. You want to look energetic and alive.

2. Take a thorough shower or bath *that day*. Pay large attention to personal hygiene. Wear deodorant. Smell fresh, but don't, please don't, wear a fragrance: no perfume, no after-shave. This didn't used to matter, but now it does. People have become hypersensitive to odors. You don't want a would-be employer praying the interview will be over soon, so they can get rid of your overpowering fragrance. And *you*. (This applies to men as well as to women.) And speaking of odors, don't forget your breath. If it sucks, you're in trouble. Just to be on the safe side, avoid onions and garlic for 24 hours before the interview; they hang around on your breath longer than you'd think. And avoid liquor that day for the same reason *(and don't think you can mask it with Listerine; it smells even worse, and in an interview any strong mouthwash virtually shouts out loud: "hey, I just had a drink")*. Instead, be sure to vigorously clean, brush, and floss your teeth, prior to going to the interview.

3. As to your clothes, colors are important. As a generalization to which there are, of course, exceptions—particularly in the techie world— employers tend to prefer candidates who don't wear a pattern, but wear

a dress or suit that is all one color, such as dark blue, light gray, brown, or black. Resist the temptation to wear something daring. During the interview, you want to call attention to yourself, not to what you're wearing. Unless you're applying for a job in creative arts or design, where creativity in your clothing may signal that you're creative also in your work. And speaking of creativity, a small splash of color—scarf, tie, handkerchief, or whatever—against the background of a solid-color suit or dress is almost always okay, in applying for any job. Women, *some* jewelry is okay. So are earrings, as long as they're not the size of a chandelier. Whatever outfit you wear, it should be freshly laundered, and if pants or a pantsuit, they should have a sharp crease.

4. Pay attention to your hair. It should be freshly cut and *modern* in its styling (especially important if you're forty years or older); and if you're a male who has hair on his face—beard or stubble—have it freshly clipped or trimmed also.

5. Watch your hands; the employer certainly will. Scrub them before the interview, and use hand lotion. Freshly trimmed fingernails, without any dirt under them, are a must. (If you're female, it's your call as to what color you paint them.) If you're carrying something in your hands—purse, folder, notebook, briefcase, or portfolio—make sure it doesn't look old. Pay attention also to your feet. Clean or manicured toenails, please, if you're wearing open-toed shoes.

A word about portfolios, since I just mentioned them. Try to think of some way to bring evidence of your skills and experience to the hiring interview. For example, if you are an artist, a craftsperson, or anyone who produces a product, try to bring a sample of what you have made or produced—in scrapbook or portfolio form, on a flash drive, on YouTube, in photos, or if you are a programmer, examples of your code. And so on.

Okay, preparation over. You're ready. Or at least as ready as you'll ever be. On to the interview!

3 DURING THE INTERVIEW

TYPES OF INTERVIEWS

The job-hunter's common picture of the job interview—before going in—is that it's going to be two people sitting down together—one, the employer, the other, you—having a conversation. And of course that's what the interview commonly is, especially if it's a small organization. Just you and her. Or just you and him.

It's also common to picture—again, ahead of time—that the interview will take place in the employer's office. And that too *sometimes* happens. But not always.

There are many more options open to an employer today about how to conduct a job interview. The types of interviews you *may* run into these days include the following:

> Face to face with a group (all at once)
> Face to face with a group (one at a time)
> Face to face with one person
> A telephone interview (audio only)
> A Skype interview (audio and video)

Let's look at each, briefly, in turn.

A TELEPHONE INTERVIEW (AUDIO ONLY)

Employers like this one. Sometimes it's the only interview, and you may—I say *may*—get hired during it. But that doesn't happen very often. Most of the time, it's only a preliminary interview, as the employer is trying to cut down the number of people they actually have to pay to fly there, or need to ask in for a more time-consuming face-to-face interview. In which case, the sole purpose of this telephone interview will be to find some reason to eliminate you. Not *hire* you. *Eliminate* you.

More often than not, if it's a larger organization, this phone interview is being conducted by the HR department, who may have only a vague idea of what the job is about, when you would rather it be an interview with the head of the department where the job is located, who actually has the power to hire you.

So, if the employer demands from the get-go that you submit to a telephone interview, be on your guard. Try to determine early on whether you're talking, or will be talking, to the HR department there, or to the boss (or a close associate of the boss).

If it's not Human Resources, great! While on the phone you want to come across as a professional, thoroughly prepared for the interview by having done detailed research on the organization beforehand, and having relevant evidence of your skills and experience—at your fingertips, while you're on the phone.

On the other hand, if you're talking to HR, keep in mind the one overriding purpose you should have, for *that* interview: *"I will try not to say anything that would get me eliminated, at this early stage."*

The best path toward this is to just be yourself, don't play games, and be as honest as you can be. Incidentally, *"I don't know"* is a perfectly legitimate answer for you to use, in response to any question they ask you, if that's the truth. Just don't say that *too* often.

FACE TO FACE WITH A GROUP (ALL AT ONCE)

You may go into the interview under the impression that it's going to be just you and her, or just you and him. And then you find it is a group of people sitting opposite you. You can just call it a crowd. But the feeling may be that it's more like a jury trial. That's understandable.

How come the crowd, and not just one individual?

Well, sometimes this is an organization committed to shared decision making in all things. And that includes hiring.

Or sometimes these interviewers are all members of the team you would be working with, and they all have a say as to whether they can work with you or not.

Or sometimes each interviewer there is a specialist in a different area of expertise, and they collectively need to check out your expertise in all those areas.

Or sometimes this is a boss who is unsure of his or her decision skills, so they've brought in others who can give them counsel and advice, based on their impressions of you.

Anyway, just relax. In the end, they're all human beings, just like you. Once upon a time they themselves may have had to sit exactly where you are now. They know what it feels like.

The crowd will not all be talking to you at once, I'm sure. It will be one by one. Just be sure that when one of them is talking, you are looking straight at that one person, not fixing your eyes on the floor or letting your gaze wander all around the room.

You've got to win this crowd over, one by one. And help them decide whether or not they like you. One by one.

And also you've got to decide whether or not you like them. One by one.

FACE TO FACE WITH A GROUP (ONE AT A TIME)

Sometimes a crowd is charged with the task of deciding whether or not to hire you, but they are sent in, one at a time, to question you in their area of expertise. This tends to be the procedure only if it's a large organization.

If you want a glimpse of this type of interview in detail, you can do no better than to browse or read the fifth edition of *Cracking the Coding Interview,* by Gayle Laakmann McDowell. (Find it online at Amazon.com, BarnesandNoble.com, or Indiebound .com.) It's for software engineers who are job-hunting, and want to interview at The Big Guys. If that's you, you'll need to be prepared for this kind of interviewing. Gayle describes it in detail, step by step, as it's practiced in various ways at Google, Yahoo!, Apple, Amazon, Facebook, and Microsoft. She is a software engineer herself, has interviewed at four of these companies, and was on the hiring committee at Google. Her book's copyright is 2013. I checked with people who know: her descriptions are really current. Of course these companies keep evolving, changing, altering. But still . . . not *that* much.

FACE TO FACE WITH ONE PERSON

This is the grand old traditional type of interview that we're all totally familiar with. If you try to find work at your local retail store, doctor's office, ranch, fast-food place, print shop, insurance company, farm, auto dealer, repair shop, etc., this is the type of interview you are going to encounter. You're more likely to be face-to-face, from the beginning, with the person who actually has the power to hire you. No intermediate layers, or steps you have to go through. As the traditional Negro spiritual[*] loudly sings, "Ain't a that a good news!"

A SKYPE INTERVIEW (AUDIO AND VIDEO)

Some employers request this kind of interview. They have their reasons. Sometimes the reasons are, shall we say, murky. But let's look at the good side. They may want to get a fuller sense of you than they can learn from just your voice. Or it may be you're in the United States, they're in Sweden (or wherever), and they can't afford to fly you there for the initial interview.

Anyway, if they ask you to do this type of interview, and you've never done it before, just type "how to do a Skype interview" into your favorite search engine. You'll get step-by-step instructions, which you can practice prior to the actual interview. You'll find that if you have a laptop with video and mike built in, you probably won't need any additional equipment. Just download the free Skype program, at www.skype.com/en/download-skype/skype-for-computer and away you go.

One word of caution: Don't get too close to the video eye in your computer, or too far away.

And try Skyping with a friend of yours who has their own computer and can download Skype if they haven't already, so they can tell you how you look and how you sound. Common pitfalls: You look a ghastly pale yellow (the lighting in the room needs to be adjusted) *and/or* the built-in video camera is not on a level with you (try putting your laptop on a pile of books, or adjusting your chair, to fix that), *and/or* you sound as if you're

---

* Or "African American spiritual" if you prefer.

talking in a cave (try speaking softer or try speaking louder; in any event, speak with energy, don't sound flat, and bored).

Okay, so much for the various types of interviews you may encounter. Now, on to what you do there.

THE BEGINNING OF THE INTERVIEW

If it's a face-to-face interview, in their building, remember to ask *everyone* you meet that day (including secretaries, receptionists, and office assistants) one simple question, if you speak with them for any length of time.

Ask if they have a business card, and if so, could you have one.

In Asian countries you don't have to ask. The business custom is to offer their business card at first meeting, held (barely) in its two upper corners by the thumb and forefinger of each hand, held out at arm's length toward you, accompanied by a deep bow.

But unless you're in a country where this is a custom, you're going to have to ask for their business card. So ask. Please. And I repeat, *do this with secretaries, receptionists, and office assistants* (who often hold the keys to the kingdom); also with any business associates there that you have any conversation with; as well as with your actual interviewer(s)—be they one or nine in number.

If any of them do not have a business card, take out your notepad or smartphone, and ask them please how to spell and pronounce their name (plus address or URL). Show them your notepad or notes on your smartphone then or later, to check what you've written; don't depend on your ears alone. What sounded like "Laura" may actually be "Lara." What sounded like "Smith" may actually be "Smythe," and so on. Get that name and address, but get it right, please. You'll have a use for these names at the end of the day.

HOW SHOULD YOU GREET THE INTERVIEWER?

Some job-hunters die at the thought of having to shake hands at an interview. Sometimes that's because disease really is running around the world these days, and they know it. In fact, they carry antiseptic wipes throughout the year, so they can stay healthy.

Other job-hunters hate the ritual of shaking hands at an interview for a different reason: they sweat buckets when they're nervous, and are sure the interviewer will notice their wet hands, and not hire them.

Well now, if your interviewer is not going to hire you because you sweat when you're nervous, *celebrate*. You didn't really want to work for that kind of place, did you? This could be a sign that they pick on every little thing there; be glad you found that out *now*, and not down the road.

But here's the overarching likelihood: most employers simply won't care. You sweat when you're nervous. So what? They've seen that, a million times before.

If it makes you feel better, carry a cotton handkerchief, and wipe your hands dry with it, just before you meet the interviewer(s).

However, if I were you, I wouldn't just assume you're going to have to shake hands at an interview. Maybe you won't. Hand-shaking is *de rigueur* in some cultures, but frowned upon in others. (That's *corporate* cultures, as well as society's.)

It is best, if you're not sure what the custom is there, to walk up to the interviewer(s), and then stop with your hands by your side, to watch and see what *they* do. If they don't extend their hand, you don't have to either. If they do extend their hand, then grasp it warmly and firmly but not wince-inducingly. Then don't drop their hand abruptly. Disengage slowly.

Smile. Say your name. Ask them their name. If in doubt that you heard it correctly, repeat what you think you heard ("was that *Megan*?"). They will correct you, if you've misheard them ("no, Regan"). Thank them: "Oh. Thanks, *Regan*." Bottom line: You may find it embarrassing to ask, but it's even more embarrassing to go through the whole interview calling them by the wrong name.

Then ask for that business card if they haven't already offered it. Read the card carefully, *there and then*. Don't just pocket it, with barely a glance. These little rituals are symbolic. *Dismiss my card, you dismiss me. Honor my card, you honor me.*

Meet the other interviewers, in turn, if there is more than one. Then sit down, wherever they indicate. We'll assume it's on a chair, not a futon. Set your butt as far back in that chair as you can, keep your feet (or at least one foot) firmly on the floor near the chair. Then lean forward, slightly. Ever so slightly. This conveys energy (always important, but most especially if you're older) and suggests you have an active interest in what's going on. This is no time to lean back and look *cool*. It's a time to focus your thoughts primarily on them, not primarily on yourself.

THE INTERVIEW IS A TWO-WAY CONVERSATION

Okay, you're seated. Now the talking begins.

Just remember, this isn't a test you're trying to pass. As we saw in the first chapter, this is a conversation. The two of you—you and "the employer"— trying to find out if you want to hang out together, for a spell. Or longer.

Okay, so what are the key concerns you should be thinking about, while this conversation is going on? Well, there are two.

Your First Key Concern in the Conversation

It's pretty basic: *"Do they like me?"*

In the job interview that means "Hey employer, you are looking for someone who can do this thing that you want done, and can get along with you and the other people here. So, given that, *do you like me?"*

You can be pretty confident they are inclined to like you if you're competent, and a professional, and have just the expertise and experience they were hoping for.

But there are some other less obvious things that will go further in helping the employer like you. Most employers will like you (or at least like you better) if you turn out to be a candidate

- who is punctual, arriving at work on time or, better yet, early; who stays until quitting time, or even leaves late;
- who is dependable;
- who has a good attitude;
- who is not afraid of hard work;
- who has drive, energy, and enthusiasm;
- who wants more than a paycheck;
- who is self-disciplined, well organized, highly motivated, and good at managing their time;
- who can handle people well;
- who can use language effectively;

- who can work on a computer;
- who is committed to teamwork;
- who is flexible, and can respond to novel situations, adapting quickly when circumstances at work change;
- who is trainable, and loves to learn;
- who is project-oriented, and goal-oriented;
- who has creativity and is good at problem solving;
- who has integrity;
- who is devotedly loyal to the organization; and
- who is able to identify opportunities, markets, and coming trends.

So, during your conversation, plan on quietly claiming any of these that you legitimately can, or even exhibit some of them during the interview if you get a bright idea as to how to do this.

(For example, if you want to claim you are punctual, prove it by arriving for the interview on time. And incidentally, "punctual" doesn't mean "way ahead of time." It means "on time." Walk around the block a couple of times if you get there too early.)

Your Second Key Concern in the Conversation

This is pretty basic, too: *"Do I like them?"*

In the job interview that means "As a prospective employee, I'd like to know if they're going to give me a work environment that will enable me to be at my most productive and most effective level, where I feel useful and appreciated, and can make a difference."

That you have this second concern, and not just the first, needs to be emphasized, underlined, and writ large, because as job-hunters so many of us are prone to think our opinion doesn't matter in the interview. I mean, maybe you need a job, any job, and you need it now; so you feel you have no business being picky.

Well, with all due respect, yes you do. Dissect that concern above, and tell me what part of it an employer — any employer — wouldn't be overjoyed to hear:

> You want to be productive, indeed, to be highly productive for that employer.
>
> You want to be effective at the task the employer is trying to accomplish.
>
> You want to be useful to that employer.
>
> And you want to make a difference for that employer's goal and bottom line.

What it all adds up to is this: this second concern of yours is not selfish or in opposition to what the employer is trying to find. It is exactly what the employer is looking for, in these interviews. So of course it's important to ask yourself if *you* like *them*.

To say the job hunt is a conversation—a two-way conversation— means your opinion matters as much as the employer's. That's always been true. And it always will be.

Now on to the actual Talking.

HOW TO DEAL WITH "TELL ME ABOUT YOURSELF"

The employer will likely be the first to ask a question, though some employers may throw the ball to you.

If you have to be the one to start, I recommend, *"I'm flattered that you invited me in for this interview. I'm very happy to be here. For starters, could you help me understand, in some detail, what this job is all about?"*

And be ready with a follow-up question: *"Okay, what* live *projects are you working on, or would I be working on, if I were hired?"*

Fine. But in most cases, not to worry; it will be the employer who starts the ball rolling. And you know what their first question is most likely to be. *"Tell me about yourself."*

It used to be that interviewers started out with this question because they weren't very good at interviewing, and this was a lame question to cover up their ignorance. That still happens with some new interviewers, of course. But now even veteran interviewers use this question. In which case, how you answer it may determine your fate during the rest of the interview.

So, here are some key points to keep in mind when answering *Tell me about yourself*:

1. In most cases, employers use this question as a kind of test. Their curiosity is, How do you respond to an open-ended, unstructured situation, the kind of challenge that life (and a job) is going to be continually presenting to you? Do you stop and take a moment or two to *think*, or do you start talking immediately and keep on gabbing endlessly, hoping inspiration will suddenly appear to light your way? Blah, blah, blah.

2. Employers generally feel you have failed the test if you respond with a question instead of an answer. Every job-hunter's favorite response—*"Well, what do you want to know?"*—is every interviewer's least favorite response. Interviewers generally interpret this to mean you knew they would be asking this, and even so, you've given absolutely no forethought to how you would answer. *A bad start!*

3. Employers are not looking for a summary of your whole life, or even a summary of your whole work life, when they ask you this question. Generally speaking, employers want to see if you can focus like a laser beam and tell them only the stuff about you that is related to this situation, this interview, and this job.* So, when you hear *"Tell me about yourself,"* imagine you are really hearing: *What experience, skills, or knowledges do you have that are relevant to the job I am trying to fill?* Because that is what the employer is really asking. Give them the answer to *that*, and you're a winner.

4. Do keep it short. One job-hunter in France had no difficulty in getting interviews, but kept getting turned down after each interview. To find out why, his counselor tried an experiment. A mock interview. Playing the employer, the counselor began, *Tell me about yourself*, and then timed him. Our job-hunter kept talking for twenty-one minutes!! Didn't even realize it! Employers expect you to have the answer well-rehearsed and brief. Yes, we're back to the elevator speech that you practiced (I hope) on page 24. I told you that you were going to need it. Now is that time. Make that your answer here.

---

* Like all generalizations, there are exceptions. Some employers like finding out from your answer to this question that they have a personal connection with you, in one way or another. It creates rapport, and they then listen to you with much more interest. But not as many employers as you think.

THE MIDDLE OF THE INTERVIEW

The middle of the interview is a free-floating conversation.

There are going to be more questions, of course. First theirs, then yours, then theirs, then yours. It has no script, and it is unpredictable. But here are a few rules that may be helpful:

Throughout the interview, determine to observe the "50-50 Rule." You shouldn't talk all the time. You shouldn't let them talk all the time, either. Experience has revealed that, in general, the people who get hired are those who divide speaking and listening fifty-fifty in the interview. People who don't follow that mix are the ones who don't get hired. Why? Nobody knows. My hunch is that if you talk too much about yourself, you come across as one who is self-absorbed and would ignore the needs of the organization; but if you talk too little, you come across as a poor communicator, or as trying to hide something about yourself. Stay 50-50.

Throughout the interview, when answering employers' questions, observe "the twenty-second to two-minute rule." Experience has confirmed that when it is your turn to speak or answer a question, you should plan not to speak any longer than two minutes at a time, if you want to make the best impression. In fact, a good answer to an employer's question sometimes only takes twenty seconds to give. (But not less than that, else you will come across as "a grunter," which means: "poor communicator.")

Throughout the interview, determine never to speak ill of a previous employer, even if they treated you horribly. It's a funny thing, but some employers feel as though they belong to a fraternity or sorority. Bad-mouthing a previous employer only makes this employer worry about what you would gossip about *them,* if they hired you.

So, plan on saying something nice about any previous employer, or if you are pretty sure it will come out that you and they didn't get along, then try to neutralize this ahead of time, by saying something simple like, *"I usually get along with everybody; but for some reason, my past employer and I just didn't get along. Don't know why. It's never happened to me before. Hope it never happens again."*

Okay, those are some of the rules.

Now, what about those other questions. Like . . .

WHAT IS YOUR GREATEST WEAKNESS?

Once they're past *Tell me about yourself,* employers can ask you a lot of other things. One expert claims there are 101 such possibilities. Another claims there are 201. Naturally, they won't all get used. But an employer can pick and choose from among them.

There is one that deserves our special attention here.

That question is, *What is your greatest weakness?*

Job-hunters freeze when they hear this. *What?!*

Unfortunately, advice from experts about how you should answer this is all over the map—from *"Take a strength—like, persistence—and claim it is a weakness"* to *"They want to see if you're honest, so confess something important that you're honestly bad at—like, 'I'm not very good at meeting deadlines.'"* (In other words, commit vocational suicide.)

The problem with all this advice is that everyone is trying to frame your answer in the language of behavior.

You should be trying to state your greatest weakness in the language of skills.

Let me illustrate. Your skills—that is, your functional or transferable skills—break down into three groups: those that you have with data and information, those that you have with people, and those that you have with things. So, look at this job in the language of skills. Ask yourself, *What are they hunting for, the most, here: my skills with people, or my skills with things, or my skills with data and information?*

Also, which family of skills are they hunting for *the least* in this job?

By way of example, let's assume you are interviewing for a job that most requires you to have excellent data/information skills, and least requires that you have skills with things.

So, pick through a list of Things skills. There must be something there that you're not good at; let's say you're lousy at *repairing stuff.* That then is what you answer, in the language of skills, when they ask for your greatest weakness. *"My greatest weakness is that I'm terrible at repairing stuff; been that way all my life."*

It's a good answer. So, give yourself an A+. Your answer is honest, it's true, and by the way, that skill/your weakness is not at all required for the job at hand.

WHAT IS A BAD EMPLOYEE?

Since the employer is worrying about any weaknesses you might have, figure out prior to the interview what weaknesses would characterize a *bad* employee there—besides the obvious things such as *comes in late, takes too much time off, follows his or her own agenda instead of the employer's,* etc. Then quietly emphasize to the employer during the interview how much you are the very opposite. Say something like: your sole goal "is to increase the organization's effectiveness, service, and bottom line."

And by the way, if you haven't a clue as to what would characterize a bad employee, then ask. During the interview. *"What would be your definition of a bad employee, for this organization? What behaviors or attitudes?"*

As for the other questions the employer may ask you during the interview, just keep in mind what I said in the first chapter. There are basically only five. To save you from looking back there, I'm going to repeat them here, together with some additional thoughts. These are the questions in an employer's mind, typically, even if they don't say them out loud.

1. **"Why are you here?"** This means, *"Why are you knocking on our door, rather than someone else's door? How much do you know about who we are, and what we do here?"* Guidelines here: Be sure to research the place to death before you go near it. Google it, look it up on LinkedIn, visit its website if it has one. Then think out what makes this place—in your eyes—superior to other places where you might work. Jot down the answers, then memorize them.

2. **"What can you do for us?"** This means, *"If we were to hire you, will you help us with the tasks and challenges we face here? What are your relevant skills, and give us examples or stories from your past that demonstrate you have these skills. Tell us about yourself."* Guidelines here: I'm assuming you are going after a particular job and you therefore know what skills the employer is looking for. If you don't, use the interview to ask, *What do you see as the skills most needed to do this job really effectively?* Then tell your stories illustrating you have such skills. Where to get your stories? If you read and did the exercises in *What Color Is Your*

Parachute? or the *What Color Is Your Parachute? Job-Hunter's Workbook,* then you use the stories you wrote when filling out the skills petal of the Flower Diagram there. On the other hand, if you didn't use either, then you must figure out ahead of time what skills this employer is looking for, and long before the interview, write out a sample story illustrating some time when you demonstrated that you have such a skill. Do this for each of the skills required, up to five in number.

3. **"What kind of person are you?"** This means, *"Will you not only fit in but actually inspire those around you? Will you be a pleasure to work with, or will you be a problem from day one? Do you have the kind of personality that makes it easy for people to work with you, and do you share the values that we have at this place?"* Guidelines here: You must demonstrate from the moment you come in the door that you have good people skills. Most employers believe "microcosm reflects macrocosm," or how you act in small matters indicates how you will act in large matters. They will notice *everything,* from how you greet the receptionist, how you make sure to include everyone in the room with your eyes when you are answering questions, etc.

4. **"What distinguishes you from, say, nineteen other people whom we are interviewing for this job?"** This means, *"What about you will give us more value for our money? What makes you unique or at least unusual; do you get more done in a day, or are you better at problem solving than others, do you have better work habits than others, do you show up earlier, stay later, work more*

thoroughly, work faster, maintain higher standards, go the extra mile, or . . . what?" Guidelines here: The answer to this concern usually lies in your traits: are you more persistent, thorough, more detailed, or what? Emphasize the appropriate traits in the telling of your stories, in point 2 above.

5. **"Can we afford you?"** This means, *"If we decide we want you here, how much will it take to get you, and are we willing and able to pay that amount—governed, as we are, by our budget, and by our inability to pay you as much as the person who would be next above you, on our organizational chart?"* Always save this discussion for as late in the interview as you possibly can. (See the first chapter and also Appendix B, "Salary Negotiation," starting on page 81, for ways to do this. And when you do get around to it, always mention a *range* of salary you're looking for, not just a single set figure.)

These are the five main things that are on an employer's mind during the interview, even if, as I said, *these five questions are never once mentioned explicitly by the employer.* These questions are still *floating* beneath the surface of the conversation, beneath all the things being discussed. Anything you can do, during the interview, to help the employer answer these five questions will help make you an outstanding candidate for the job.

Of course, it's not just the employer who has questions in the interview. You have questions too, remember? I repeat here, again, the list we first saw in the first chapter; these are the essential five questions you should be trying to figure out, during the interview:

1. **"What does this job involve?"** *You want to under-stand exactly what tasks will be asked of you, so you can determine if these are the kinds of tasks you would really like to do, and can do. One way to probe this is to ask, "If you decide to hire me, what kind of live problem or task would I be working on here?"*

2. **"What are the skills and experience a top employee in this job should ideally have?"** *You want to find out if your skills match those that a top employee in this job has to have, in order to do this job well. Problem: Many employers who have the power to hire you don't at all understand the actual job they're hiring for, even though it's in their department. (I kid you not.)*

3. **"Are these the kinds of people I would like to work with, or not?"** *Do not ignore your intuition if it tells you that you would not be comfortable working with these people! You want to know if they have the kind of per-sonalities that would enable you to accomplish your best work. If these people aren't it (and you aren't yet desper-ate), keep looking! Being surrounded by energy-drainers will kill your enthusiasm for going to work. (Vampire movies are popular for a reason.) Keep your eyes open. Pay attention.*

4. **"If we like each other, and want to work together, can I persuade them there is something unique about me that makes me different from, say, nineteen other people they are interviewing for this job?"** *You need to think out, way ahead of time, what does make you different from other people who can do the same job. For example, if you are good at analyzing problems, how do you do that? (1) Painstakingly? (2) Intuitively, in a flash? (3) By consulting with greater authorities in*

the field? You see the point. You are trying to put your finger on the "style" or "manner" in which you do your work that is distinctive, and hopefully appealing, to this employer, so that they choose you over other people they are interviewing.

5. **"Can I persuade them, at the end, to hire me at the salary I need or want?"** *Covered in Appendix B.*

HOW AM I DOING, SO FAR?

And that's it! Don't make the middle of the interview any more complicated than it needs to be.

But do check yourself along the way, by making the following observations mentally:

First of all, quietly notice the time frame of the questions the employer is asking you, because if things are going favorably for you, the employer's questions should move through the following five time stages.

1. Questions about the distant past: *e.g., "Where did you attend high school?"*

2. Questions about the immediate past: *e.g., "Tell me about your most recent job."*

3. Questions about the present: *e.g., "What kind of a job are you looking for?"*

4. Questions about the immediate future: *e.g., "Would you be able to come back for another interview next week?"*

5. Questions about the distant future: *e.g., "Where would you like to be five years from now?"*

The more the time frame of the interviewer's questions moves from the past toward the future, the more favorably you may assume the interview is going for you. On the other hand, if the interviewer's questions always stay firmly in the past, this is a bad sign.

Time to Describe the Job

But let's be optimistic. Let's assume the time frame of the interviewer's questions moves firmly into the future. Then what? Well, then it is time for you to get more specific about the job in question. Experts say it is essential for you to ask at that point these kinds of questions, if you haven't already:

- If I were hired, what duties would I be performing?
- What would you be wanting me to accomplish?
- What responsibilities would I have?
- Would I be working individually, or as a member of a team, or group?
- To whom would I be reporting? (*Remember, the communication skills and personal warmth of an employee's supervisor are often crucial in determining the employee's tenure and performance. In fact, recent research shows that the quality of the supervisor may be more important than the experience and individual attributes of the workers themselves.*)
- Whose responsibility is it to see that I get the training I need, here, to get up to speed?
- How would I be evaluated, how often, and by whom?
- What were the strengths and weaknesses of previous people in this position?
- Can you tell me a live problem or challenge you would want me to handle, if you hire me?

- May I meet the persons I would be working with and for (if it isn't you)?

Indulge Your Curiosities

Even if you're not sure how things are going, there are some curiosities it is always appropriate for you to ask the employer about:

- What characterizes the most successful employees this company has?
- What significant changes has this company gone through in the past five years?
- What future changes do you see in the work here?
- Whom do you see as your allies, colleagues, or competitors in this business?
- What values are sacred to this company?

In sum, ask anything you're curious about, unless you can imagine a likely response will be *"That's none of your business."* Don't even think of asking *that kind* of question.

Your Impressions

A job interview isn't all questions. No, for the umptieth time: It's a conversation, and during that conversation you can and should volunteer your impressions, too:

- Tell them what you **like** about this organization.
- Tell them what sorts of **challenges** you find intriguing—in this field in general, and in this organization in particular.
- Tell them what **skills** seem to you to be necessary in order to meet such challenges, and mention that you have them. Do remember that in these days of "behavioral interviews" employers are looking for

concrete *examples* from your past performance and achievement—your behavior—of skills you claim to have, not just vague statements like, "I'm good at . . ."

- You should already have figured out *"What are the three most important competencies that this job requires?"* But if you haven't figured that out by now, then be sure to pose that question. Then, of course, concentrate particularly on those three, and demonstrate that you have them (one hopes) with some of your stories.

By the way, face the fact that you're probably going to make mistakes during the interview. (You'll kick yourself later, when you realize what they were.) But don't fret! Mistakes are expected. You don't have to get it right all the time. They want a human, not a robot. You can use a thank-you note that night, to correct any false impressions you think you may have left behind you.

On the off chance that you ever run into an employer who will not forgive a mistake you made during the interview, I have one question for you: why on earth would you want to work in a place like that? Let them go.

THE CLOSING OF THE INTERVIEW

If this interview is not to be your last one there, they will tell you so. Indeed, with larger organizations it can be assumed, these days, that it will be a series of interviews there.

This is evidenced in two modern-day rules that experts will teach you about interviews and resumes:

1. *The sole purpose of a resume is to get yourself invited in for an interview.*

2. *The sole purpose of an interview is to get yourself invited back for another interview.*

So being invited back for another interview—and then another—is a good thing. But eventually you will come to an end; the end of the final interview there. Assuming you have decided that you like them and maybe they like you, there is one question you should not fail to ask:

"Can you offer me this job?"

I know this sounds like a fairy tale, but in fact many job-hunters have secured a job simply by being bold enough to ask for it, at the end of the (final) interview.

I don't know why this is. I only know that it is. So after hearing all about this job at this place, if you decide you'd really like to have it, you must ask for it. The worst thing the employer can say is "No," or "We need some time to think about all the interviews we're conducting."

IF THEY SAY NO

You are of course not too happy, especially if you really, really wanted this job. But your time there wasn't wasted if you ask them before you go out the door, **"Can you think of anyone else who might be interested in my skills and experience?"** They may have valuable colleagues who they know to be hiring, or who might in turn know of someone else who is looking for someone with your gifts and experience. Link to link to link.

IF THEY SAY MAYBE

"We need more time" can be understood to be a *maybe*. And if you just leave it there, you will leave them in control of your fate. To keep this in your control, not theirs, there are three questions you should follow up with:

1. **"When may I expect to hear from you?"** If the employer says, "We need some time to think about this," or "We will be calling you for another interview," you don't want to leave this as a vague good intention on the employer's part. You want to nail it down. So you should persist:

2. **"Might I ask what would be the latest I can expect to hear from you?"** The employer has probably given you their best guess, in answer to your previous question. Now you want to know: what is the worst-case scenario? Once you have found it out, ask them the next question in this sequence:

3. **"May I contact you after that date, if for any reason you haven't gotten back to me by that time?"** Some employers resent this question. You'll know that is the case if they snap at you. But a decent employer will appreciate your offering them what is in essence a safety net. They know they can get busy, become overwhelmed with other things, forget about you. It's reassuring, in such a case, for you to offer to rescue them.

Be sure to jot down right in front of them any answers they give you to these three questions, so they will see you are taking them seriously; then stand up, give a firm handshake, with eye contact, thank them sincerely for their time, and leave.

In the following days, rigorously keep to all that you said, and don't contact them except with that mandatory thank-you note, until after the latest deadline you two agreed upon, in answer to question 2. You don't want to be seen as a pest. But if you do have to contact them after that date, maybe they will give you some good news. If they don't, and if they tell you things are still up in the air, you should gently ask questions 1, 2, and 3, all over again.

IF THEY SAY YES: POSSIBLE JOB OFFERS FROM THE EMPLOYER

Well, that's the astonishing thing that can happen, if you build up your courage and ask them at the end of the interviewing, *Can you offer me this job?* They may say Yes right on the spot. More likely, if it's a committee that is interviewing you, they may need time to huddle and compare notes. Still they may end up saying Yes further down the road.

So what if they do say *Yes?*

Most often, their Yes is attached to a specific kind of job offer. There are at least four kinds of offers an employer can make to you.

Full-Time Work Offer

Full-time work is variously defined. It used to be "40 hours a week," but the Affordable Care Act now defines full time as 30 hours a week or more. There are a number of benefits, including health care, that are only available to full-time employees. *Or,*

Part-Time Work Offer

Part time is any number of hours that is less than full time. This may range from one to twenty-nine hours per week. This may be the best an employer can offer, at the moment, and if you were hoping for a full-time job, you will have to decide whether to accept this, or to keep looking. *Or,*

Project Work Offer

This has to do not so much with hours per week as *to* how many weeks (or months) the job will last. The employment will end when the project is completed. *Or,*

Zero-Hour Work Offer

Popular in the United Kingdom but likely to spread, this is a written statement that specifies a person is an employee of the organization, and agrees to be ready for work if and when they are needed, but the organization is under no obligation to provide work for them, nor is the employee obligated to take a particular assignment, when offered. It is essentially a loose "on call" arrangement. The employee is paid only for the hours actually worked, not for the hours "on call." A recent survey in the U.K. discovered that the average number of hours worked by those with zero hours contracts was 19.5 hours per week.[*] So it ends up being a part-time work offer.

You will need, in any case, to determine whether the employer (and the government) thinks you are an employee or an independent contractor. The distinction is important. If you don't know why, then explore it before you go into the interview.[**]

Whatever they offer, decide whether you want to take it or not. Do salary negotiation and discussion of benefits, please (see Appendix B). And then if you decide to take it,

Get It in Writing

When this is all done—the discussion of the job, the job offer, the salary negotiation, and the concluding discussion of

---

[*] An August 5, 2013, survey by the Chartered Institute of Personnel and Development (CIPD) in the U.K. (www.cipd.co.uk).

[**] See http://jobsearch.about.com/od/employmentlaw/a/employee.htm. Allison Doyle is (always) an excellent source of information on her About.com Job Searching site.

benefits—then you want to get everything they've offered summarized, *in writing*. In writing (or typed) and *signed*.

The reason? Many employers unfortunately "forget" what they told you during the hiring interview, or even deny they ever said such a thing. It shouldn't happen; but it does.

Sometimes it's true: they honestly forgot what they said. Other times, of course, they're playing a game. Or their successor is, who may disown any *unwritten* promises you claim they made to you at the time of hiring. They may respond with, *"I don't know what caused them to say that to you, but they clearly exceeded their authority, and of course we can't be held to that."*

I repeat: get it all in writing. And signed. It's called a letter of agreement—or employment contract. If it is a small employer (ten or fewer employees), they may not know how to draw one up. If you're on the Internet or have a friend who is, put the search term "sample letter of agreement between employer and employee" into your favorite search engine, and you'll get lots of free examples. I particularly like the one from Inc.com. You or the employer can write this up. Then they should sign it. You too. With dates.

You have every right to ask for this. If they simply won't give it to you, *beware*.

At-Will Employment

Most letters of agreement or employment contracts are for what is called "at-will employment." The "will" is the employer's will. What this means is the employer has the right to let you go at any time, without any warning, and without having to specify any cause or reason. Fortunately, not all hiring agreements are for at-will employment. But do ask if this one is.

Some employers will specify conditions under which termination is forbidden, in fact some states require that it be specified, and some union contracts require it also, if you're working in a place that's been unionized.

Normal reasons for which you can't be fired: age, race, sexual orientation, ethnic background, religious beliefs, civil rights violations, or if you have filed for workers' compensation; also if you have reported wrongdoing by your employer to legal authorities. But naturally, there are loads of ways that clever employers can get around any and all of these, if they try hard. So, just stay vigilant.

In drawing up the hiring contract, you should ask if the organization has a written policy about termination, or specifies a procedure that must be followed, before an employee may be lawfully terminated, such as can be found in the organization's employee manual, if they have one. Small companies may or may not. Large organizations always will.

4 AFTER THE INTERVIEW

THE THANK-YOU NOTE OR NOTES

You're home. It's over. Things aren't settled yet, so you're probably going to have to go back for another interview. But at least this one is done and gone. Time to put up your feet and relax. Except . . . Oh, how I hate to interrupt this little fantasy. But don't start relaxing just yet. You've got work to do.

Every expert on interviewing will tell you two things:

1. Thank-you notes *must* be sent after every interview, by every job-hunter; but

2. Most job-hunters ignore this advice.

Indeed, it is safe to say this is the most overlooked step in the entire interviewing process.

Says one human resources expert: *"A prompt, brief . . . letter thanking me for my time along with a (brief!) synopsis of his/her unique qualities communicates to me that this person is an assertive, motivated, customer-service-oriented salesperson who utilizes technology and knows the rules of the 'game.' These are qualities I am looking for. . . . At the moment I receive approximately one such letter . . . for every fifteen candidates interviewed."*

You want to distinguish yourself from, say, nineteen other people who are interviewing for that job? Send thank-you notes. That day, that same night—to everyone you met there, that day. That's assuming you remembered to ask everyone you met that day for their business card, or name and email address, at the least.

When you write, no need to ramble on and on. Your thank-you note can be just two or three sentences. Something like: *"I wanted to thank you for talking with me today. It was very helpful to me. I much appreciated your taking the time out of your busy schedule to see me. Best wishes to you,"* and then sign it.

Nice to do, but not really necessary? *No, no, no.* Make that *essential!* I have talked to numerous job-hunters over the years who were told by their employer that the reason they got hired was because they were the only one who took the time and trouble to send a thank-you note.

If you need any additional encouragement to send thank-you letters (besides the fact that it may get you the job), here are six more reasons for sending a thank-you note, especially to those who interviewed you:

First, you were presenting yourself as one who has good skills with people. Your actions with respect to the job interview must back this claim up. Sending a thank-you note does that. The employer can see you are good with people; you remember to thank them.

Second, it helps the employer recall who you are. Very helpful if they've interviewed a dozen people that day.

Third, if several people will be involved in the hiring decision, but only one of them was at this particular interview, the man or woman who interviewed you today has something to show the others, particularly if you used the thank-you note to summarize the main points you discussed.

Fourth, if the interview went rather well, and the interviewer(s) showed an interest in further talks, you can use the thank-you note to reiterate *your* interest in having those further talks.

Fifth, the thank-you note gives you an opportunity to correct any wrong impression you left behind. And, you can add anything you forgot to tell them that you wanted them to know. Moreover, from among all the things you discussed you can underline the two or three points that you want most to stand out in their minds.

Lastly, if the interview did not go well, or you lost all interest in working there, and this thank-you note is sort of "goodbye and thanks," keep in mind that they may hear of openings elsewhere that would be of interest to you. In the thank-you note, you can mention this, and ask them to please let you know if they hear of anything anywhere. If these were kind men and women who interviewed you, they may indeed send you some leads over the next few weeks.

IF YOU GOT THE JOB: KEEP ON JOB-HUNTING

No, I don't mean if you *didn't* get hired. I mean, if you *did*.

It shouldn't happen, but it does. Interviewed on Tuesday. Hired on Wednesday. Told to report for work on the following Monday.

But . . . on Monday or before, you get a phone call saying that the job just isn't going to happen, after all. The possible reasons are many: They sold the company. There's a serious crisis in the world. The boss had a heart attack over the weekend. A big contract on which you were going to be working just collapsed. In any event, the bottom line is that you're back out pounding the pavement. So, get a head start against this eventuality. Don't discontinue your job search just because you have a job offer. There's many a slip 'twixt the cup and the lip.

IF YOU DIDN'T GET THE JOB: WHY YOU DIDN'T

Don't get discouraged if you get turned down after your interview there. Job expert Tom Jackson[*] accurately described the job-hunt as a series of interviews that end like this:

NO NO NO NO NO NO NO NO NO NO NO NO
NO NO NO NO NO NO NO NO NO NO NO NO
NO YES YES

Every NO you get out of the way, you're one step closer to YES.

You're of course trying to figure out why you didn't get hired. Well, that's something you may never be able to find out. But I can generalize from what I have learned over forty years, and tell you why a lot of job-hunters didn't get hired in the past. Maybe there's some wisdom here for you:

1. **Nervous mannerisms. It is a turnoff for many employers if**

   - you continually avoid eye contact with the employer (in fact, this is a big, big no-no); or

---

[*] Author of *The Perfect Resume: Today's Ultimate Job Search Tool* (Broadway Books, 2004).

- you give a limp handshake; or

- you slouch in your chair, or endlessly fidget with your hands, or crack your knuckles, or constantly play with your hair during the interview.

2. **Lack of self-confidence. It is a turnoff for many employers if**

- you are speaking so softly you cannot be heard, or so loudly you can be heard two rooms away; or

- you are giving answers in an extremely hesitant fashion; or

- you are giving only one-word answers (no, yes, maybe, not yet, I think so) to all the employer's questions; or

- you are constantly interrupting the employer; or

- you are downplaying your achievements or abilities, or are continuously being self-critical in comments you make about yourself during the interview.

3. **The consideration you show to other people. It is a turnoff for many employers if**

- you show a lack of courtesy to the receptionist, secretary, and (if at lunch) to the waiter or waitress; or

- you display extreme criticalness toward your previous employers and places of work; or

- you drink strong stuff during the interview process. I mentioned this earlier: no alcohol. That includes while you're still with the employer. If the employer takes you to lunch, you must never order a drink, even if the employer does—this, in an abundance of caution. Ordering a drink raises the question in the employer's mind, *"Does he/she normally stop with one, or do they normally keep on going?"* Don't . . . do . . . it! . . . even if they do; or

- you forget to thank the interviewer as you're leaving, or forget to send that mandatory thank you note.

4. **Your values. It is a complete turnoff for many employers, if they see in you**

- any sign of arrogance or excessive aggressiveness; any sign of tardiness or failure to keep appointments and commitments on time, including this interview; or

- any sign of laziness or lack of motivation; or

- any sign of constant complaining or blaming things on others; or

- any signs of dishonesty or lying—especially on your resume or during the interview; or

- any signs of irresponsibility or tendency to goof off; or

- any sign of not following instructions or obeying rules; or

- any sign of a lack of enthusiasm for this organization and what it is trying to do; or

- any sign of instability, inappropriate response, and the like; or

- other ways in which you evidence your values, such as: what things impress you or don't impress you in their office; or what you are willing to sacrifice in order to get this job and what you are not willing to sacrifice in order to get this job; or your enthusiasm for work; or the carefulness with which you did or didn't research this company before you came in; and blah, blah, blah.

Incidentally, many an employer will watch to see if you smoke, either in the office or at lunch. In a race between two equally qualified people, the nonsmoker will win out over the smoker 94 percent of the time, according to a study done by a professor of business at Seattle University. Sorry to report this, but there it is!

So, there you have it: these are the reasons other job-hunters lost the interview. Notice that these reasons have nothing to do with your ability to do that job. It reminds us of a basic truth. The interviewer is not just looking at your competencies. They're looking at you. The whole You.

APPENDIX A
HANDICAPS

YOU ARE HANDICAPPED, EH? EVERYONE IS HANDICAPPED

I know what you're thinking. You're thinking that if you get turned down in the interview, it won't be for any of the reasons I've just cited. No, it will be because you have some handicap (*hidden or obvious*) that makes you unemployable.

You're thinking, I got turned down (or *I will be turned down*) because

> I have a physical disability *or*
> I have a mental disability *or*
> I never graduated from high school *or*
> I never graduated from college *or*
> I am just graduating *or*
> I just graduated two years ago and am still
>   unemployed *or*
> I graduated way too long ago *or*
> I am too beautiful or handsome *or*
> I am too ugly *or*

I am too fat *or*

I am too thin *or*

I am too old *or*

I am too young *or*

I am too near retirement *or*

I have only had one employer in life *or*

I have hopped from job to job all my life *or*

I have been out of the job market too long *or*

I have been in the job market far too long *or*

I am too inexperienced *or*

I am an ex-con or felon *or*

I have a psychiatric history *or*

I have not had enough education and am
    underqualified *or*

I have too much education and am overqualified *or*

I am Hispanic *or*

I am Black *or*

I am Asian *or*

My English is not very good *or*

I speak heavily accented English *or*

I am too much of a specialist *or*

I am too much of a generalist *or*

I am ex-clergy *or*

I am a returning vet *or*

I am too assertive *or*

I am too shy *or*

I have only worked for volunteer organizations *or*

I have only worked for small organizations *or*

I have only worked for a large organization *or*

I have only worked for the government *or*

I come from a very different culture or background *or*

I come from another industry *or*

I come from another planet.

Now, if all you can think of as you're going into the interview is your handicap, and all you can think of while you're in the interview is your handicap, and you are wondering as you look at each interviewer what they think of your handicap and how much they're bothered by it, then I can guarantee you one thing: it isn't your handicap that is keeping you from getting hired; it is your preoccupation with it.

I'd like to free you from that obsession. You'll enjoy the interviews much more.

So, let's get one thing straight, from the beginning here: you can't possibly have a handicap that will keep employers from hiring you. You can only have a handicap that will keep *some* employers from hiring you. I said *only some*.

No matter what handicap you have, or think you have, it cannot possibly keep you from getting hired anywhere in the world. It can only keep you from getting hired *at some places* in the world.

You must learn to think of all employers as divided into two tribes: employers who are interested in hiring you for *what you can do*; vs. employers who are bothered by *what you can't do*. There are both kinds, out there.

But you should only be looking for those obsessed with what you *can* do. And that had better be your obsession, too. Else it will be *your attitude* that kills your chances of getting hired; not the handicap itself.

Obsessing about, worrying about, your supposed handicap imports a certain loneliness into the interview. You feel like the blue zebra amid all the elephants on an African plain. "Among all the people they are interviewing today, I and I alone am handicapped." That is a terrible feeling, and it will affect your interview; so dump it, real quick.

Preoccupy your thoughts, instead, with this fundamental truth: everyone is handicapped.

And I mean: *everyone*.

REAL HANDICAPS: WHAT YOU CAN'T DO AND WHAT YOU CAN DO

Think about the meaning of the word "handicap." Its alternative name is *dis-ability*: its opposite is *ability*.

So, consider how many abilities—which is to say, skills—there are in the world. Actually, no one knows that number, so let's make one up. Let's say there are **4,341 transferable skills** in the whole world.

How many of those 4,341 do you think the average person has? No one knows that number either, so let's again make one up. Let's guess *big* here. Let's guess the average person has **1,341** transferable skills. That means there are 1,341 things the average worker **can** do. You know, things like *dig, analyze, communicate, sell, design, cook, repair*—those sorts of things.

But if there are 4,341 abilities in the world, and the average person only has 1,341 of them, then that leaves 3,000 abilities the average person doesn't have. We don't normally use the long, cumbersome phrase "abilities I don't have." We call them instead "dis-abilities." The average person, by this calculation, has 3,000 dis-abilities.

Of course, what those 3,000 are, will vary from person to person. But, in the end, *everybody* is handicapped. Everyone has dis-abilities. Everyone is disabled, in some sense. Everybody.

So, you are not in splendid solitude when you're sitting in the interview(s). You're a person with some abilities and some dis-abilities sitting with others who all have abilities and dis-abilities. It's just a question of *which?*

If your dis-abilities (the things you can't do) are not abilities required in the particular job you're interviewing for, then who cares that you are supposedly handicapped? For these people who are interviewing you, there are jobs they can't do, either. They're not dwelling on the fact that they too are handicapped. So when they interview you, all they want to know is what you *can* do, not what you *can't.* Their question to you: "Can you do the things I need to have done on the job we're talking about?"

What you can do is the proper conversation of the interview. What you can't do is not a proper discussion, unless it affects the requirements of the job.

Focus your attention on what you can do. This should help: take a piece of paper, online or off, and divide it into two columns, viz:

I have this skill:	I don't have this skill:

Then, look at this famous *List of 246 Skills as Verbs*, on the next pages:

achieving	acting	adapting	addressing	administering
advising	analyzing	anticipating	arbitrating	arranging
ascertaining	assembling	assessing	attaining	auditing
budgeting	building	calculating	charting	checking
classifying	coaching	collecting	communicating	compiling
completing	composing	computing	conceptualizing	conducting
conserving	consolidating	constructing	controlling	coordinating
coping	counseling	creating	deciding	defining
delivering	designing	detailing	detecting	determining
developing	devising	diagnosing	digging	directing
discovering	dispensing	displaying	disproving	dissecting
distributing	diverting	dramatizing	drawing	driving
editing	eliminating	empathizing	enforcing	establishing
estimating	evaluating	examining	expanding	experimenting
explaining	expressing	extracting	filing	financing
fixing	following	formulating	founding	gathering
generating	getting	giving	guiding	handling
having responsibility	heading	helping	hypothesizing	identifying
illustrating	imagining	implementing	improving	improvising
increasing	influencing	informing	initiating	innovating
inspecting	inspiring	installing	instituting	instructing
integrating	interpreting	interviewing	intuiting	inventing
inventorying	investigating	judging	keeping	leading
learning	lecturing	lifting	listening	logging
maintaining	making	managing	manipulating	mediating
meeting	memorizing	mentoring	modeling	monitoring
motivating	navigating	negotiating	observing	obtaining

offering	operating	ordering	organizing	originating
overseeing	painting	perceiving	performing	persuading
photographing	piloting	planning	playing	predicting
preparing	prescribing	presenting	printing	problem solving
processing	producing	programming	projecting	promoting
proofreading	protecting	providing	publicizing	purchasing
questioning	raising	reading	realizing	reasoning
receiving	recommending	reconciling	recording	recruiting
reducing	referring	rehabilitating	relating	remembering
rendering	repairing	reporting	representing	researching
resolving	responding	restoring	retrieving	reviewing
risking	scheduling	selecting	selling	sensing
separating	serving	setting	setting up	sewing
shaping	sharing	showing	singing	sketching
solving	sorting	speaking	studying	summarizing
supervising	supplying	symbolizing	synergizing	synthesizing
systematizing	taking instructions	talking	teaching	team building
telling	tending	testing & proving	training	transcribing
translating	traveling	treating	trouble-shooting	tutoring
typing	umpiring	understanding	understudying	undertaking
unifying	uniting	upgrading	using	utilizing
verbalizing	washing	weighing	winning	working
writing				

Copy as many of the skills from the list above as you want into the proper column, depending on whether you *can* do the skill, or you *cannot*. (*Not yet, anyway.*)

Now when you are done, meditate on what you put in the *Can* column. Pick out five favorite things that you *can* do, and *love* to do; and write out some brief story of how you actually did *that*, sometime in your past—for each of the five.

Returning vets: I'm talking particularly to *you*.

PHANTOM HANDICAPS: ONLY IN THE EYES OF SOME EMPLOYERS

It is important for you to understand that the word "handicap" is a broad term, which doesn't necessarily refer to something going on in your life. It may, in fact, refer to something going on in the life of the employer.

Suppose you cannot hear, even with the best technical augmentation. If you are considering a job that requires acute hearing—say, working in the back room of a radio station—then that is a genuine dis-ability: because there are certain skills essential for *that* job that you just don't have.

But now let us suppose you can hear perfectly, but you are way overweight. Your overweight is not a dis-ability for that job in the back room of that radio station, because it would not interfere with your ability to do that job.

Still you may get turned down, not because you can't do the job but because that particular employer is prejudiced against overweight people. You can't say that being overweight is a handicap, at least not for that job.

HANDICAP VS. PREJUDICE

You're dealing with something else here: not a dis-ability but a prejudice. So mark this difference well: a **dis-ability** is a statement about *you*. A **prejudice** is a statement about *that employer*.

Both may technically be called handicaps, in the sense that both *may* keep you from getting hired in this interview—at least with some employers—but it is important to understand that *a real handicap* is a disability you have—you cannot do some important task required in that particular job. On the other hand, an employer's prejudice is *a phantom handicap*. It may raise its ugly head in one particular interview or more, but if you keep on going, find an employer who only cares whether you can do the job or not, then poof! the so-called handicap vanishes.

You must just be sure this prejudice remains the sole possession of that employer. Don't you buy into it. That is, don't look at yourself through *their* eyes. Look at yourself through your own eyes.

If you can do the job, keep going until you find an employer who is not prejudiced about your being overweight. Or whatever.

THE KEY EMPLOYER PREJUDICES

1. The employer prejudice that is currently getting all the attention relates to **how long you've been out of work**. It is a prejudice that some employers have, and some employers don't. If you've been out of work a year or more, you will find employers who won't hire you because of it. Some, not all. Too bad for them! Just keep going until you find employers who don't have that prejudice.

2. The next employer prejudice that you may run into is **age**. Reason? Millions of baby boomers (*the 76 million people born 1946–1964*) are entering the so-called retirement years. You might get turned down after the interview because you are too old. But again, your comfort lies in the fact that this is a prejudice, not a handicap: some employers won't be prejudiced that you are as old as you are, if they see you are still on fire with passion about what you do, what you *can* do, not merely marking time between now and then.

3. The related employer prejudice that is rearing its ugly head these days concerns **money**. Given all a baby boomer's years of working, many older workers expect a salary befitting all their years of experience and wisdom, only to discover that some employers are prejudiced against paying them that much— since the employer could hire two less experienced workers in their twenties for what it would cost them to hire just one baby boomer.

4. Next employer prejudice: **ex-offenders**. When you run into any employer prejudice, what you should do is Google it by name on the Internet, and see what you turn up. You may discover some very useful resources, advice, or strategies, including what to do in an interview. The most detailed help I know of, for ex-offenders who are interviewing, is found on the website run by a man named Dick Gaither. Let me tell you about him. He is head of Job Search Training Systems in Indiana, and has worked with ex-offenders a lot, over many years. Email Dick at workwizard@ aol.com and he will send you 126 pages of useful information and guidance that you can print out. Incredibly helpful, and . . . *it's free*. A great public service, from a tremendous human being.

5. Next employer prejudice: **former mental or psychiatric patients**. The same comments that I made in #4 apply here.

6. **Others**. There is hardly a group you can name who does not face *some* prejudice from *some* employers.

With all these prejudices, one basic fact stands out: you will run into employers who are good and kind, and then again, you will run into employers who aren't. Keep going, until you find the good and kind ones.

Personally, I draw comfort from all the employers I run into who are a credit to the human race. Here is a letter I got from a successful job-hunter* just last week:

> "As we went along in the interview, some of the things the employer told me were, 'I'm very flexible with schedules. I want to put people in activities that I know they'll be the best in, but that means that some weeks you're scheduled for three evening shifts. If that's ever a problem, I really want you to tell me, because I can fix it. I'm also a firm believer that you need to be at your absolute best before you can pour into people here. That means, if you get really stressed out, I want you to tell me. Just yesterday one of our employees came to me and said, "I'm so overwhelmed right now!" So I sat down with her and we moved some stuff around. Now, that also means that we are extremely team-oriented. If someone cannot take a shift because something is going on at home, everyone needs to be willing to take that up sometimes. But, you always know that everyone here is willing to do the same for you. Also, when we're stressed we seem to resort to silliness.' I knew immediately that this was the place for me. . . ."

*Kayla DeVitto.

APPENDIX B
SALARY NEGOTIATION

If and when the interviewer says Yes, we really do want you, and you reply Yes, I really want to work here, then and only then is discussion of salary appropriate.

Unfortunately, salary discussion isn't what it was prior to 2008. Ever since the Great Recession ended, employers have tended to hang tougher on the question of salary, less yielding, more unbending, than they used to be. In many sectors of the economy currently there is less room for salary negotiation.

But then, that's the way it always is: during times when unemployment is low, it's a job-hunter's market, but when unemployment is (relatively) high, then it's an employer's market.

But once a job offer has been made to you, and only then, you may want to try doing some salary negotiation anyway. It will help a lot if you know what you're doing. So here are the four secrets you need to know.

THE FIRST SECRET OF SALARY NEGOTIATION

The Purpose of Salary Negotiation Is to Uncover the
Most That an Employer Is Willing to Pay to Get You

Negotiation. There's the word that strikes terror into the hearts of most job-hunters or career-changers. Why do we have to negotiate?

Simple. It would never be necessary if every employer in every hiring interview were to mention, right from the start, the top figure they are willing to pay for that position. A few employers do. And that's the end of any salary negotiation. But most employers don't.

They know, from the beginning of the interview, the top figure they're willing to pay for this position under discussion. But. But. They're hoping they'll be able to get you for less. So they *start* the bidding (*for that is what it is*) lower than they're ultimately willing to go.

And this creates a range.

A range between the lowest they're hoping to pay vs. the highest they can afford to pay. And that range is what the negotiation is all about.

For example, if the employer can afford to pay you $30 an hour, but wants to try to get you for $18 an hour, the range is $18–$30.

You have every right to try to negotiate the highest salary that employer is willing to pay you, *within that range*.

Nothing's wrong with the goals of either of you. The employer's goal is to save money, if possible. Your goal is to bring home to your own household the most money that you can, for the work you will be doing.

THE SECOND SECRET OF SALARY NEGOTIATION

During Salary Discussion, Never Be the First One to
Mention a Salary Figure

I've been saying this throughout this little guide. Never negotiate or attempt to negotiate until a job offer has actually been made or is about to be. Where salary negotiation has been successfully kept offstage for much of the interview process, when it finally does come up, there is one important idea you should keep in your mind: and that is, you never want to be the first one to mention a salary figure. Believe me, you want the employer to be the first one to mention a figure, if you possibly can.

Why? Nobody knows. It's just been observed over the years that where the goals are opposite, as in this case—you are trying to get the employer to pay the most they can, and the employer is trying to pay the least they can—whoever mentions a salary figure first generally loses. We don't know *why* that is; we just know it is.

Inexperienced employers/interviewers often don't know this strange rule. But experienced ones are very aware of it. That's why *they* will try to get you to mention a figure first, by asking you some innocent-sounding question, like: *"What kind of salary are you looking for?"*

Well, how kind of them to ask me what I want—you may be thinking. No, no, no. Kindness has nothing to do with it. They are hoping you will be the first to mention a figure, because they know this summary of thousands of interviews in the past: *whoever mentions a salary figure first generally loses the negotiation, in the end.*

Accordingly, if they ask you to be the first to name a figure, you want to have a simple countermove, at the ready. The simplest is often the best: "Well, you created this position, so you must have some figure in mind, and I'd be interested in first hearing what that figure is."

THE THIRD SECRET OF SALARY NEGOTIATION

Research the Range That the Employer Likely Has in Mind, and Then Define an Interrelated Range for Yourself, Relative to the Employer's Range

Now this is a bit complicated, and you may not have the time to figure this out. But you ought to at least know how this works, either for this job-hunt or for your next one.

It begins by thinking through what your goal is here. You do not want to be discussing a salary *figure* here. You want to be talking back and forth in terms of salary *ranges*.

First, the employer's, the range of what they could offer you. In any organization that has more than five employees, that range is comparatively easy to figure out. It will be less than what the person who would be above you makes, and more than what the person who would be below you makes. Examples:

If the Person Who Would Be Below You Makes	And the Person Who Would Be Above You Makes	The Range for Your Job Would Be
$45,000	$55,000	$47,000–$53,000
$30,000	$35,500	$32,500–$34,000

One teensy-tiny little problem here: how do you find out the salary of those who would be above and below you? Well, I hate to tell you, but it means *research*. If you just love doing research, you'll be in seventh heaven here. But if you hate it, then this approach isn't going to be of much interest to you.

Okay, research. Research *what?*

Well, referring to the preceding diagram, in the organization that interests you, begin by finding out the names of the people above and below you, or at least the names of their positions.

If it is a small organization you are going after—one with twenty or fewer employees—finding out this information should be easy. Any employee who works there is likely to know the answer. Since up to two-thirds of all new jobs are created by small companies of this size, that's the kind of organization you are likely to be researching, anyway.

On the other hand, if you are going after a larger organization, then you fall back on a familiar life preserver, namely, *every* person you know (family, friend, relative, business, or spiritual acquaintance) and ask them who they know that might know the company in question and, therefore, the information you seek.

In either case—large organization or small—once you've found out who you need to talk to, then use your own personal bridge-person—someone who knows you and also knows them—to get an introduction.

LinkedIn should prove immensely helpful to you here, in locating such people. If you're not already on it, get on it (www .LinkedIn.com).

So should a site called Jobs with Friends (http://friends .careercloud.com).

Maybe this will turn out to be easier than you thought it was going to be. And then again, maybe it won't. It's possible you'll run into an absolute blank wall at a particular organization that interests you (everyone who works there is pledged to secrecy, and they have shipped all their ex-employees to Siberia). And online salary sites in this case turn out not to be helpful, at all. In that case, seek out information *on their nearest competitor* in the same geographic area. For example, let us say you were trying to find out managerial salaries at Bank X, and that place was proving to be inscrutable about what they pay their managers. You would then turn to Bank Y as your research base, to see if the information is easier to come by there. And if it is, you can assume the two may be basically similar in their pay scales, and that what you learned about Bank Y is probably applicable to Bank X.

Note: In your salary research take note of the fact that most governmental agencies have civil service positions paralleling those in private industry—and government job descriptions and pay ranges are available to the public. Go to the nearest city, county, regional, state, or federal civil service office, find the job description nearest the kind of job you are seeking in private industry, and then ask the starting salary.

When this is all done, you turn to the employer's range. See the chart with which we began here. Suppose you guess that the employer's range for the kind of job you're seeking is $36,500 to $47,200. Before you go in for the interview, you figure out an "asking" range for yourself, which you're going to use when the interview gets to the salary negotiation part.

And here's where it gets a little tricky. Your minimum asking range should "hook in" just below that employer's maximum, and then go up from there. If the employer chooses the minimum in your range (maybe, maybe), that will turn out to be the maximum within their range.

The diagram here shows how this works:

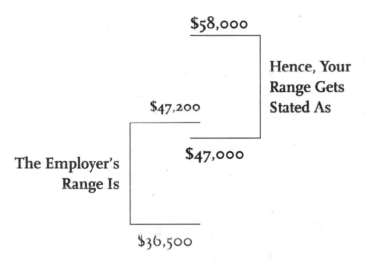

$58,000

Hence, Your
Range Gets
Stated As

$47,200

$47,000

The Employer's
Range Is

$36,500

So much for the research. Now, at the end of the interview(s) if they have made you a job offer, then the employer will state a figure (probably around the bottom of their range, let us say in this case, $36,500). Thanks to your research, you will be ready to respond with something along these lines: *"I understand, of course, the constraints under which all organizations are operating these days, but I am confident that my productivity is going to be such, that it will justify a salary"*—and here you mention *your* range, as calculated above—where your bottom figure starts just below the top of their range, and goes up from there—*"in the range of $47,000 to $58,000."*

It will help a lot during this discussion, if you are prepared to show in what ways you will make money or in what ways you will save money for that organization, such as would justify this higher salary you are asking for. Even if they accept your offer at the bottom of your range, you are still near the top figure they're willing to pay.

Yes, it's clever. Yes, it takes some work. And yes, there's no guarantee whatsoever that it will work. But it may. In which case, you will feel rewarded for going the second mile in this part of the interview.

Okay, but suppose it doesn't work. What if the employer has a ceiling they have to work with, and it's below what you're asking, and you're dying to work there? What if—to make this possibility even more grim—you just cannot live on what they're offering? What then?

Well, as career expert Daniel Porot suggests, you can try offering them part of your time, leaving you free to go find additional income elsewhere.

How does this work? Let's say you need, and believe you deserve, $50,000 annually, but they can only offer you $30,000. In which case, since $30,000 over $50,000 is $3/5$, you might consider offering them three days of a five-day workweek for that $30,000 they are offering. If they say okay, this leaves you free to take work elsewhere during those other two days, not to mention the weekend.

You will of course determine to produce so much work during those three days per week you are there that they will be ecstatic about this bargain—wouldn't you be? *Almost* a fulltime worker for only $3/5$ of the cost?

Try it. The worst thing they can say is no.

THE FOURTH SECRET OF SALARY NEGOTIATION

Know How to Bring the Salary Negotiation to a Close; Don't Leave It "Just Hanging"

Salary negotiation with this employer is not finished until you've addressed more than salary. Unless you're an independent contractor,[*] you want to talk about so-called fringe benefits. "Fringes" such as life insurance, health benefits or health plans, vacation or holiday time, and retirement programs typically add anywhere from 15 to 28 percent to many workers' salaries. That is to say, if an employee receives $3,000 salary per week, the fringe benefits are worth another $450 to $840 per week.

So, before you even walk into the interview you should decide what benefits are at the top of the list for you. And then, after the basic salary discussion is settled, you can go on to ask them what benefits they offer there and be ready to fight for *those*. In this tough economy, the employer may not yield. But it's worth it, to gently, gently try.

Good luck and Godspeed.

---

[*] For the IRS's explanation of this, see http://www.irs.gov/Businesses/Small-Businesses-&-Self-Employed/Independent Contractor Self Employed or Employee.

ABOUT THE AUTHOR

Dick Bolles—more formally known as Richard Nelson Bolles—is the author of *What Color Is Your Parachute? A Practical Guide for Job-Hunters and Career-Changers*, the most popular job-hunting book in the world. The book has sold more than ten million copies to date, and is dramatically updated, reshaped, and rewritten, every year, in English. "Parachute," as it's often called, has been translated into twenty languages and is used in twenty-six countries. Dick is credited with founding the modern career counseling field, and is often described as the field's #1 celebrity.

What Color Is Your Parachute? was chosen as one of the 100 All-TIME best and most influential nonfiction books published since 1923, by *Time* magazine.

It was chosen as one of twenty-five books that have shaped people's lives (down through history) by the Library of Congress's Center for the Book.

It was chosen as one of the books since 1758 that have helped shape the world of work, by the United States Department of Labor.

Dick Bolles was chosen by *Forbes* magazine as one of the "Wealth Wizards" in the United States (along with Warren Buffett and eighteen others), for all the jobs he has helped create.

He is the recipient of the National Samaritan Award (previous honorees include Karl Menninger, Betty Ford, and Peter Drucker).

He has his own websites: www.jobhuntersbible.com and www.eParachute.com. He has a public Facebook page: www.facebook.com/dick.bolles.1.

He is also one of LinkedIn's 500+ "Influencers" and writes regularly for that platform, as well as for Google+ and a number of others.

He is the father of four grown children: Stephen, Sharon, Gary, and Mark (deceased). He also raised a stepdaughter, Serena, in a former marriage. He and his wife, Marci, live in the San Francisco Bay Area.

INDEX

U

Unemployment
    prejudice related to, 77
    salary negotiation and, 81

V

Vacation time, 89
Values, importance of, 66–67
Veterans, 76

W

Weaknesses, questions about,
    45–47
Websites
    of employers, 15
    for salary research, 23–24,
    85

Z

Zero-hour work offers, 58

ADDITIONAL HELPFUL RESOURCES FROM THE AUTHOR

What Color is Your Parachute? 2014
The best-selling job-hunting book in the world by Richard N. Bolles

Trade Paperback ISBN: 9781607743620
eBook ISBN: 9781607743644

The Job-Hunter's Survival Guide
A quick guide for when time is of the essence by Richard N. Bolles

Trade Paperback ISBN: 9781580080262
eBook ISBN: 9780307759429

**What Color Is Your Parachute?
Job-Hunter's Workbook,
Fourth Edition**
A fill-in edition of the famous Flower Exercise by Richard N. Bolles

Trade Paperback ISBN: 9781607744979

**What Color Is Your Parachute?
Job-Hunter's Workbook,
Tablet Edition**
An interactive edition for your iPad and Nook by Richard N. Bolles

iPad ISBN: 9781607745792
Nook ISBN: 9781607746041

Visit JobHuntersBible.com and eParachute.com